S0-CFG-711

Cézanne
IN PROVENCE

Pomegranate

SAN FRANCISCO

Pomegranate Communications, Inc.
Box 808022, Petaluma CA 94975
800-227-1428; www.pomegranate.com

Pomegranate Europe Ltd.
Unit 1, Heathcote Business Centre, Hurlbutt Road
Warwick, Warwickshire CV34 6TD, UK
[+44] 0 1926 430111; sales@pomeurope.co.uk

ISBN 0-7649-3627-1
Pomegranate Catalog No. AA323

Pomegranate publishes books of postcards on a wide range of subjects.
Please contact the publisher for more information.

Cover designed by Mariah Lander
Printed in Korea

15 14 13 12 11 10 09 08 07 06   10 9 8 7 6 5 4 3 2 1

To facilitate detachment of the postcards from this book, fold each card along its perforation line before tearing.

The son of a banker in Aix-en-Provence, Paul Cézanne, along with his friends, spent idyllic days of childhood lying under great pine trees; exploring the ruins of a Roman aqueduct; swimming and fishing in the River Arc; or climbing the rocky canyons to the Zola Dam and the foothills of Montagne Sainte-Victoire. The ancient history and natural beauty of the land became part of the artist's persona.

Cézanne pursued his passionate desire to become an artist despite paternal disapproval. After studying drawing and flirting with a career in law, he made several trips to Paris in the 1860s. There he studied the work of old masters such as Veronese, Tintoretto, and Rubens, and the modern giants Eugène Delacroix and Gustave Courbet, and met young impressionist painters, such as Edouard Manet, Claude Monet, and Camille Pissarro. Under Pissarro's influence, Cézanne learned to use a lighter range of color, to vary his brushwork, and to paint outdoors. When his father died in 1886, leaving him a legacy, Cézanne returned to his native Aix, where he spent most of his last twenty years.

Although he experimented with impressionist techniques in the 1870s, he soon grew impatient with them and reached instead for a more formal, structured style. An emotional man, he found stability in the painted depiction of nature, especially in the familiar countryside around his native

Aix-en-Provence. In 1886 Cézanne referred to his birthplace as "this country, which has not yet found an interpreter worthy of the riches it offers."

At the end of his life Cézanne built a studio on the outskirts of Aix, where he painted a series of Bathers, considered by many to be his crowning achievement. From Aix, Cézanne wrote to fellow artist Emile Bernard, "I have sworn to die painting," a vow he fulfilled, for he was found outdoors after a cold autumn rainstorm, lying unconscious beside his easel. He died a few days later at the age of 67.

The images collected here are from the exhibition Cézanne in Provence—organized by the National Gallery of Art, Washington, the Musée Granet and the Communauté du Pays d'Aix, Aix-en-Provence, and the Réunion des musées nationaux, Paris—the principal international exhibition marking 2006 as the centenary of the death of Paul Cézanne (1839–1906).

Cézanne in Provence

Paul Cézanne (French, 1839–1906)
Château Noir, 1900–1904

Oil on canvas, 73.7 x 96.6 cm
National Gallery of Art, Washington
Gift of Eugene and Agnes E. Meyer 1958.10.1

BOX 808022   PETALUMA   CA 94975

Pomegranate

Cézanne in Provence

Paul Cézanne (French, 1839–1906)
Mont Sainte-Victoire (La Montagne Sainte-Victoire), ca. 1902

Oil on canvas, 83.8 x 65.1 cm
The Henry and Rose Pearlman Foundation; on long-term
loan to the Princeton University Art Museum

BOX 808022   PETALUMA   CA 94975

Pomegranate

Cézanne in Provence

Paul Cézanne (French, 1839–1906)
The Viaduct at L'Estaque, 1882

Oil on canvas, 46.5 x 55.6 cm
Allen Memorial Art Museum, Oberlin College, Oberlin, Ohio.
R. T. Miller, Jr. Fund and Mrs. F. F. Prentiss Fund, 1950.3

BOX 808022 PETALUMA CA 94975

Pomegranate

Cézanne in Provence

Paul Cézanne (French, 1839–1906)
The Artist's Father, Reading "L'Événement," 1866

Oil on canvas, 198.5 x 119.3 cm
National Gallery of Art, Washington
Collection of Mr. and Mrs. Paul Mellon 1970.5.1

BOX 808022   PETALUMA   CA 94975

Pomegranate

Cézanne in Provence

Paul Cézanne (French, 1839–1906)
House and Dovecote at Bellevue, 1890–1892

Oil on canvas, 65 x 81 cm
Museum Folkwang, Essen

BOX 808022   PETALUMA   CA 94975

Pomegranate

Cézanne in Provence

Paul Cézanne (French, 1839–1906)
The Gulf of Marseille Seen from L'Estaque, c. 1876–1879

Oil on canvas, 58 x 72 cm
Private Collection, Musée d'Orsay, Paris, gift to the
French nation (with life interest retained), 2000

BOX 808022   PETALUMA   CA 94975

Pomegranate

Cézanne in Provence

Paul Cézanne (French, 1839–1906)
Houses in Provence: The Riaux Valley near L'Estaque, c. 1883

Oil on canvas, 65 x 81.3 cm
National Gallery of Art, Washington
Collection of Mr. and Mrs. Paul Mellon 1973.68.1

BOX 808022   PETALUMA   CA 94975

Pomegranate

Cézanne in Provence

Paul Cézanne (French, 1839–1906)
The Bibémus Quarry, c. 1895

Oil and canvas, 65 x 81 cm
Museum Folkwang, Essen

BOX 808022   PETALUMA   CA 94975

Pomegranate

Cézanne in Provence

Paul Cézanne (French, 1839–1906)
Cardplayers, 1890–1899

Oil on canvas, 47 x 55.9 cm
Musée d'Orsay, Paris,
Bequest of the Comte Isaac de Camondo, 1911

BOX 808022   PETALUMA   CA 94975

Pomegranate

Cézanne in Provence

Paul Cézanne (French, 1839–1906)
The Garden at Les Lauves (Le Jardin des Lauves), c. 1906

Oil on canvas, 65.4 x 81 cm
Acquired 1955
The Phillips Collection, Washington, DC

CA 94975

PETALUMA

BOX 808022

Pomegranate

Cézanne in Provence

Paul Cézanne (French, 1839–1906)
Montagne Sainte-Victoire, c. 1887

Oil on canvas, 66.8 x 92.3 cm
The Samuel Courtauld Trust, Courtauld Institute of Art Gallery, London

BOX 808022 PETALUMA CA 94975

Pomegranate

Cézanne in Provence

Paul Cézanne (French, 1839–1906)
Madame Cézanne in the Conservatory, 1891–1892

Oil on canvas, 92.1 x 73 cm
Lent by The Metropolitan Museum of Art,
Bequest of Stephen C. Clark, 1960 (61.101.2)

BOX 808022   PETALUMA   CA 94975

Pomegranate

Cézanne in Provence

Paul Cézanne (French, 1839–1906)
Maison Maria with a View of Château Noir, c. 1895

Oil on canvas, 65 x 81 cm
Kimbell Art Museum

BOX 808022   PETALUMA   CA 94975

Pomegranate

Cézanne in Provence

Paul Cézanne (French, 1839–1906)
Large Bathers, 1894–1905

Oil on canvas, 127.2 x 196.1 cm
The National Gallery, London

Pomegranate

BOX 808022   PETALUMA   CA 94975

Cézanne in Provence

Paul Cézanne (French, 1839–1906)
The Bend in the Road, 1902–1906

Oil on canvas, 82.1 x 66 cm
National Gallery of Art, Washington
Collection of Mr. and Mrs. Paul Mellon 1985.64.8

Pomegranate

BOX 808022   PETALUMA   CA 94975

Cézanne in Provence

Paul Cézanne (French, 1839–1906)
The Gulf of Marseille Seen from L'Estaque, c. 1885

Oil on canvas, 73 x 100.3 cm
Lent by The Metropolitan Museum of Art,
H. O. Havemeyer Collection,
Bequest of Mrs. H. O. Havemeyer, 1929 (29.100.67)

BOX 808022   PETALUMA   CA 94975

Pomegranate

Cézanne in Provence

Paul Cézanne (French, 1839–1906)
Montagne Sainte-Victoire Seen from Montbriand, 1882–1885

Oil on canvas, 65.4 x 81.6 cm
Lent by The Metropolitan Museum of Art,
H. O. Havemeyer Collection,
Bequest of Mrs. H. O. Havemeyer, 1929 (29.100.64)

BOX 808022   PETALUMA   CA 94975

Pomegranate

Cézanne in Provence

Paul Cézanne (French, 1839–1906)
Still Life with Milk Jug and Fruit, c. 1900

Oil on canvas, 45.8 x 54.9 cm
National Gallery of Art, Washington
Gift of the W. Averell Harriman Foundation
in memory of Marie N. Harriman 1972.9.5

Pomegranate

BOX 808022   PETALUMA   CA 94975

Cézanne in Provence

Paul Cézanne (French, 1839–1906)
Forest, 1902–1904

Oil on canvas, 81.9 x 66 cm
National Gallery of Canada, Ottawa, Purchased 1950

BOX 808022   PETALUMA   CA 94975

Pomegranate

Cézanne in Provence

Paul Cézanne (French, 1839–1906)
Still Life with Apples and Peaches, c. 1905

Oil on canvas, 81 x 100.5 cm
National Gallery of Art, Washington
Gift of Eugene and Agnes E. Meyer 1959.15.1

BOX 808022   PETALUMA   CA 94975

Pomegranate

Cézanne in Provence

Paul Cézanne (French, 1839–1906)
The Bibémus Quarry, 1896–1897

Oil on canvas, 65 x 54 cm
Private Collection

BOX 808022   PETALUMA   CA 94975

Pomegranate

Cézanne in Provence

Paul Cézanne (French, 1839–1906)
Man in a Blue Smock, c. 1896–1897

Oil on canvas, 81.5 x 64.8 cm
Acquired in memory of Richard F. Brown, the Kimbell Art Museum's first
director, by the Kimbell Board of Trustees, assisted by the gifts of many friends

BOX 808022   PETALUMA   CA 94975

Pomegranate

Cézanne in Provence

Paul Cézanne (French, 1839–1906)
Road in Provence, 1890–1892

Oil on canvas, 63.6 x 79.5 cm
The National Gallery, London

Pomegranate

BOX 808022   PETALUMA   CA 94975

Cézanne in Provence

Paul Cézanne (French, 1839–1906)
The Peppermint Bottle, 1893–1895

Oil on canvas, 65.9 x 82.1 cm
National Gallery of Art, Washington
Chester Dale Collection 1963.10.104

BOX 808022   PETALUMA   CA 94975

Pomegranate

Cézanne in Provence

Paul Cézanne (French, 1839–1906)
Chestnut Trees at the Jas de Bouffan in Winter, 1885–1886

Oil on canvas, 71.1 x 90.2 cm
Lent by The Minneapolis Institute of Arts,
The William Hood Dunwoody Fund

BOX 808022   PETALUMA   CA 94975

Pomegranate